Ride it BMX

Rachel Stuckey

 Crabtree Publishing Company

www.crabtreebooks.com

Created by Bobbie Kalman

Author
Rachel Stuckey

Project coordinator
Kathy Middleton

Editors
Molly Aloian
Kathryn White

Proofreader
Wendy Scavuzzo

Photo research
Melissa McClellan

Design
Tibor Choleva
Melissa McClellan

Production coordinator
Margaret Amy Salter

Prepress technician
Margaret Amy Salter

Print coordinator
Katherine Berti

Consultant
Matt Wilhelm

Illustrations
Leif Peng: page 9

Photographs
Shutterstock.com: © Timothy Large (front cover); © Sue McDonald (toc page, p 4);
© Timothy Large (pp 5 top, 10, 12); © homydesign (pp 14, 25); © Igor Jandric
(p 15 bottom); © Andrew Park (p 18); © Michel Stevelmans (p 20); © Andrey
Khrolenok (p 22 right); © K. Thorsen (p 24); © Jorg Hackemann (p 31 top);
© spotmatik (p 31 bottom)
iStockphoto.com: © Catherine Lane (p 5 bottom); © Robert Anderson (p 15 top)
Fotolia.com: © Simon Zoltán (p 16)
Thinkstock: Photodisc (p 6); iStockphoto (pp 7, 21); Zoonar (p 19 left)
Dreamstime.com: © Ermess (titlepage); © Danredrup (pp 11, 23); © Peter Kim
(pp 17, 28); © Brian Finestone (p 19 right); © Daniel Oberbillig (p 22 left);
© Ang Wee Heng John (p 30) / Corbis: © Troy Wayrynen/ NewSport (p 26);
Tony Donaldson /Icon SMI (p 27) / © Sabbath Photography (back cover, p 13);
Photorapher's Direct: © Phil Seale (p 31) / © Kathy Wilhelm (p 29)

Created for Crabtree Publishing by BlueApple*Works*

Library and Archives Canada Cataloguing in Publication

Stuckey, Rachel
      Ride it BMX / Rachel Stuckey.

(Sports starters)
Includes index.
Issued also in electronic format.
ISBN 978-0-7787-3150-4 (bound).--ISBN 978-0-7787-3161-0 (pbk.)

      1. Bicycle motocross--Juvenile literature. I. Title.
II. Series: Sports starters (St. Catharines, Ont.)

GV1049.3.S78 2012   j796.6'22   C2012-900870-2

Library of Congress Cataloging-in-Publication Data

Stuckey, Rachel.
      Ride it BMX / Rachel Stuckey.
         p. cm. -- (sports starters)
      Includes index.
      ISBN 978-0-7787-3150-4 (reinforced library binding : alk. paper) --
      ISBN 978-0-7787-3161-0 (pbk. : alk. paper) -- ISBN 978-1-4271-8848-9
      (electronic pdf) -- ISBN 978-1-4271-9751-1 (electronic html)
      1. Bicycle motocross--Juvenile literature. I. Title.
      GV1049.3.S78 2012
      796.6'22--dc23
                                                    2012004030

Crabtree Publishing Company

Printed in the U.S.A./032012/CJ20120215

www.crabtreebooks.com   1-800-387-7650

Copyright © **2012 CRABTREE PUBLISHING COMPANY**. All rights reserved. No part of this publication may be reproduced, stored in a retrieval system or be transmitted in any form or by any means, electronic, mechanical, photocopying, recording, or otherwise, without the prior written permission of Crabtree Publishing Company. In Canada: We acknowledge the financial support of the Government of Canada through the Canada Book Fund for our publishing activities.

Published in Canada
Crabtree Publishing
616 Welland Ave.
St. Catharines, Ontario
L2M 5V6

Published in the United States
Crabtree Publishing
PMB 59051
350 Fifth Avenue, 59th Floor
New York, New York 10118

Published in the United Kingdom
Crabtree Publishing
Maritime House
Basin Road North, Hove
BN41 1WR

Published in Australia
Crabtree Publishing
3 Charles Street
Coburg North
VIC 3058

Contents

What is BMX?

BMX is an exciting type of bicycle riding. BMX stands for bicycle motocross. Motocross is motorcycle racing on dirt tracks. Bicycle motocross is the human-powered version! The bicycles used in motocross racing are called BMX bikes. BMX bikes are smaller than other bicycles. They have sturdy frames and small wheels. They are easier to ride than larger bikes.

The bicycles used in motocross racing are called BMX bikes.

Riding it

In Freestyle BMX, riders do tricks on their bikes. BMX tricks can be done on flat ground, **half-pipes**, ramps, and outdoor trails. BMX racing uses tracks with jumps and other obstacles.

BMX racing uses tracks with jumps.

Stingray

The Stingray was a bike made by Schwinn in the 1960s. It had a banana-shaped seat, high handlebars, and 20-inch (51 cm) wheels. The Stingray looked more like a motorcycle than other bicycles. Kids in California used their Stingrays to race like motocross. That was the beginning of BMX!

Helmets and leathers

It is important to wear long pants and long-sleeved shirts when racing BMX bikes. Competitive racers wear special suits called **leathers**. BMX racers also wear gloves, pads, and special shoes. A **full-face helmet** is a must! For safety, a BMX racing bike has no kickstand or reflectors on it. And racers make sure the bolts on their bikes are tight!

Competitive racers also wear goggles to protect their eyes.

Tricks on pegs

BMX freestylers wear helmets, as well as ankle and shin pads. It is best to wear comfortable clothes and shoes when doing tricks. Some freestyle BMX bikes have special pegs on the **wheel axles**. Flatland riders stand on these pegs when doing tricks.

A flatland BMX rider stands on his bike's pegs and **balances** *on his rear wheel.*

peg

Start your motos!

A BMX track has jumps, bumps, and turns. **Tabletop jumps** are flat on top. A **whoop-de-whoop** is a rounded bump in the track. **Berms** are turns that rise up the side of the track. A **straightaway** is a straight section where riders can **sprint** to build their speed. All BMX tracks have starting gates at the top of a **slope**. The slope helps racers build **momentum**.

At the track

Only eight riders at a time compete in a race. Trial races are called **motos**. The winner of each moto gets to compete in the final race. BMX tracks hold races for all ages and skill levels.

finish

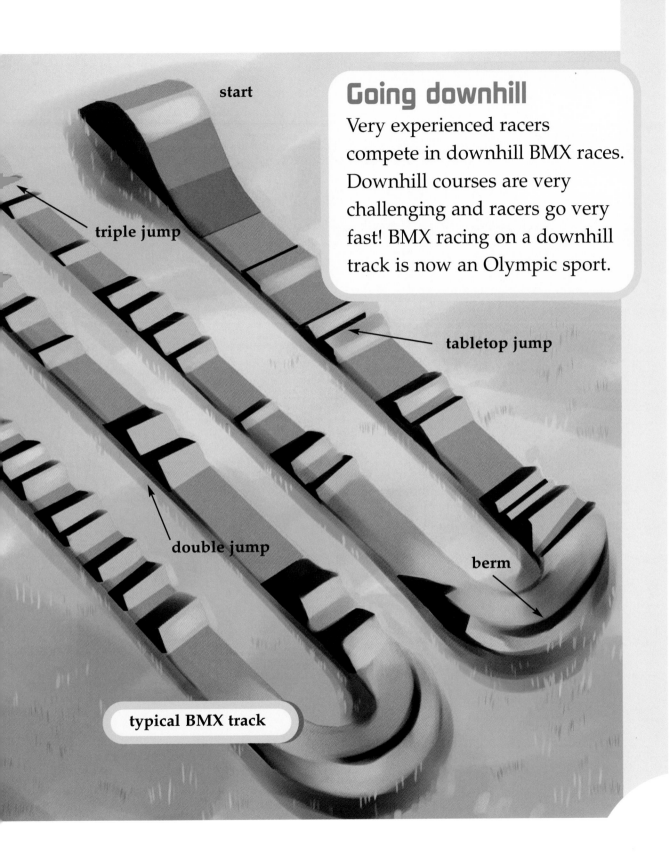

start

triple jump

Going downhill

Very experienced racers compete in downhill BMX races. Downhill courses are very challenging and racers go very fast! BMX racing on a downhill track is now an Olympic sport.

tabletop jump

double jump

berm

typical BMX track

Riders at the gate!

The start is the most important part of a BMX race. Riders must practice their start more than any other move in the race. Riders begin at the gate—a small fence that drops when the race begins. Riders line up their bikes against the gate. Beginners start with one foot on the ground and one foot on a pedal. Experienced riders balance with both feet on the pedals.

These BMX riders are waiting for the gate to drop.

Riders start a BMX race by pedaling down a slope.

Riders ready

BMX races use a recording called a **cadence**, which tells riders that the race is about to start. Once they hear "Riders ready...Watch the gate," riders must be ready to go! Lights that look like traffic lights flash and riders hear loud beeps. Then the gate drops! The start gate on a BMX track is at the top of a slope. The riders use the hill to help them build momentum. When the gate drops, the riders pedal as fast as they can down the slope. If a rider has a slow start, he or she will fall behind.

Excuse me

BMX racing is a sprint. The riders start in a straight line. But after the start, the track narrows and riders must use **strategy** to get ahead of the pack. Riders can **collide** when trying to pass, so they must also be cautious when racing. A rider can use berms to pass the other riders.

Riders use a berm to try to pass other riders.

The lead rider on a straightaway cannot do anything to prevent another rider from passing.

Passing through

There are different ways to take a berm. A rider can go high or outside on the rise to get around other riders. A rider can also stay low and inside to stop other riders from passing. **Railing**, or riding straight through the middle of a berm, allows a rider to maintain speed. He or she can then try to pass other riders on the straightaway. On the final stretch—the straightaway at the end of the course—the lead rider is not allowed to do anything to prevent other riders from passing.

Flying free

There are different types of freestyle BMX. In Park BMX, riders do tricks in special parks called skateparks. Skateparks are built with ramps and bowls and other obstacles for skateboarders and BMX riders. Sometimes skateparks also have half-pipes. Doing tricks on a half-pipe is called vert BMX. BMX riders use speed, momentum, and gravity to do tricks on a half-pipe. They fly through the air!

A rider practices tricks in a skatepark.

High jumps

In Trail BMX, riders do tricks on outdoor trails with jumps built from dirt.

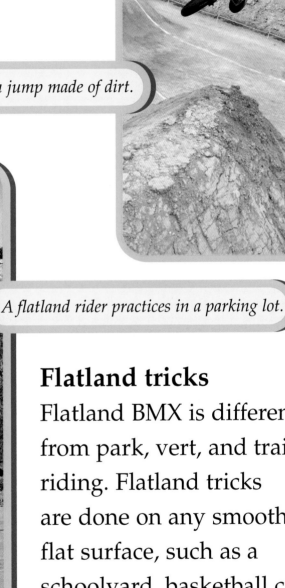

A BMX rider takes a jump made of dirt.

A flatland rider practices in a parking lot.

Flatland tricks

Flatland BMX is different from park, vert, and trail riding. Flatland tricks are done on any smooth flat surface, such as a schoolyard, basketball court, or parking lot. Flatland does not use any tracks or ramps.

Dirty jumps

Trail riders jump over packs on the trail.

Trail BMX is done on outdoor trails with sets of jumps called packs. A 4-pack has 4 jumps, one right after the other. Some tracks have 6-packs or 8-packs. Each jump has a steep take off called a **lip**. Trail riders often build their own jumps. Riders must land smoothly and be ready to take the next jump. Flow and style is important in trail BMX.

How high?

Dirt jumping is a type of trail BMX. Riders use very steep jumps to fly very high into the air and perform crazy tricks. The higher they go, the more complicated their tricks. Dirt jumping first began as a sideshow at racing events. Riders would do stunt jumps between races.

Dirt jumpers do some crazy tricks!

In and out of a bowl

Vert BMX comes from the word "vertical." Vert tricks are done high in the air above a **half-pipe** or a bowl. A half-pipe is a long ramp that looks like the letter C on its side. A bowl is a big hole with slopes all around it. Riders begin at the top and ride down one slope to build speed. They can then pedal up the other side until they are **airborne**.

A rider performs tricks in a skatepark bowl.

Getting air!

Aerials are tricks done in the air. When riders complete a full turn, they are doing a spin. The best riders can rotate their bikes in the air two and a half times.

Flatlands

Flatland riders do not use ramps or jumps to perform their tricks.

Flatland BMX is a special kind of freestyling. Flatland riders do not use ramps or trails to do their tricks. Instead of using gravity, flatland riders must build their own momentum to complete their tricks. Flatland riders design **routines** for competition. In competitions, riders cannot touch the ground with their feet. To maintain their balance, riders must keep moving.

Performing on pegs

A flatland BMX bike has pegs attached to its wheel axles. Riders balance on these pegs when performing tricks. BMX bikes used for flatland are stronger than racing and other freestyle bikes. The pegs must be strong enough to hold the rider's weight when doing tricks. Wheelies, tailwhips, and rockwalks are just some of the tricks beginners can learn. Each one requires balance and flexibility!

A BMX rider completes a tailwhip.

Stay low

While BMX freestylers aim high, BMX racers should stay low. The goal of racing is to finish first, so BMX riders must go fast. Riders lose speed whenever their wheels are in the air.

BMX racers have to learn how to fall safely, too.

Bails and Dabs

When first learning freestyle tricks, riders must learn how to bail or fall off their bikes safely. Freestylers begin to learn tricks by touching one foot to the ground or dabbing.

BMX racers must be careful to not land on top of a jump.

Jumping for speed

It takes a lot of practice to jump low to the ground. Riders must raise their front wheel as they ride up a jump, then land their back wheel on the downslope of the jump. Sometimes they land on top of a jump by mistake. This is called casing a jump. Casing will slow down a rider. And it can be a shock!

Rules and judges

In BMX racing, the first rider past the finish line wins. Most BMX tracks have the same rules because they belong to BMX associations. For safety, you must never go the wrong way on a BMX track and you must always follow the directions of the race organizers and track managers. Riders always race in their own age division. In each age division, there are three experience levels: beginner, novice, and expert. You must win races to move from one level to the next.

BMX tracks have races for all ages and skill levels.

A flatland rider completes his routine.

It's all about style

Freestyle competitions have judges that award points for creativity, skill, and style. There are no specific requirements in the different types of freestyle BMX. Each type of competition has its own rules. For example, flatland riders cannot touch the ground with their feet during a routine.

Competition

BMX races are held all over the world. Local tracks run races for all age groups and levels. BMX associations follow international rules governing BMX racing. Riders must win a series of races to progress to the final. Winners of the final race usually get trophies. The BMX World Championships are held each year around the world.

BMX races are held all over the world.

Brian Foster floats a 360 over the middle of the BMX Park course at the X Games XV in Los Angeles, California.

Extreme games

Local BMX clubs and groups organize freestyle competitions. The best riders compete in national and international events. The most popular freestyle competitions are the X Games in the United States. There are many different categories in the X Games. Other "extreme" games and BMX events are held all over the world.

Stars

There are many famous BMX riders, from racers to freestylers. Dave Mirra, known as the "Miracle Boy," is the most successful ramp rider in the world. He has won more X Games medals than any other competitor and even has his own video game. He invented and improved many BMX tricks.

Dave Mirra during the Dew Tour BMX park competition.

Matt Wilhelm is a flatland rider. He has won two national titles, three X Games medals, and a silver medal in the World Championships. He can spin on a BMX bike faster than anyone else in the world.

Champions

One of the most successful BMX racers in the world is Randy Stumpfhauser from California. He has won more medals at the BMX World Championships than anyone else. But BMX racing isn't just for boys! Girls and women have been racing BMX since the early days. Gabriela Diaz of Argentina is one of the most successful racers. In 2008, Maris Stromberg of Latvia and Anne-Caroline Chausson of France won the first Olympic Gold Medals for BMX.

Ride it!

Bike riding is a great way to have fun and stay active. BMX bikes are sturdy and small—they are easy to ride! But freestyle BMX and BMX racing require a lot of practice and training. You can start by getting on your BMX bike and going for a ride. Visit your local skatepark—many have special times for BMX riders only. Join a local club or sign up for a clinic.

Look for a BMX track in your area. Every age and skill level is welcome. Many tracks have coaching for beginners. When starting out, take it slow. Watch other racers and practice on the course. Race day is an all-day event for the whole family!

Always wear your helmet and other protective gear.

When you are ready to start racing or freestyling, be sure to ride in a safe place!

Start by getting on your bike and going for a ride!

Glossary

Note: Boldfaced words that are defined in the text may not appear in the glossary.

airborne To be in the air after taking off from the ground

balances Stays upright and steady

cadence A voice recording that signals the start of a BMX race

collide To bump into each other while moving

full-face helmet A helmet that covers the whole head, including the face

half-pipes Long two-sided ramps that look like pipes cut in half

leathers Protective suit worn by motocross and BMX riders

lip The steep take-off slope of a dirt jump

momentum The building up of speed

routines A prepared plan of tricks and moves

slope A surface where one side is higher than the other

sprint Going very fast for a short period of time

strategy A plan for completing a task

wheel axles The center rod that a wheel spins around

Index